Mendocino County Bookmobile
105 N. Main St.
Ukiah, CA 95482

CELEBRATING HOLIDAYS

Veterans Day

by Rachel Grack

BELLWETHER MEDIA • MINNEAPOLIS, MN

Note to Librarians, Teachers, and Parents:

Blastoff! Readers are carefully developed by literacy experts and combine standards-based content with developmentally appropriate text.

Level 1 provides the most support through repetition of high-frequency words, light text, predictable sentence patterns, and strong visual support.

Level 2 offers early readers a bit more challenge through varied simple sentences, increased text load, and less repetition of high-frequency words.

Level 3 advances early-fluent readers toward fluency through increased text and concept load, less reliance on visuals, longer sentences, and more literary language.

Level 4 builds reading stamina by providing more text per page, increased use of punctuation, greater variation in sentence patterns, and increasingly challenging vocabulary.

Level 5 encourages children to move from "learning to read" to "reading to learn" by providing even more text, varied writing styles, and less familiar topics.

Whichever book is right for your reader, Blastoff! Readers are the perfect books to build confidence and encourage a love of reading that will last a lifetime!

This edition first published in 2018 by Bellwether Media, Inc.

No part of this publication may be reproduced in whole or in part without written permission of the publisher. For information regarding permission, write to Bellwether Media, Inc., Attention: Permissions Department, 5357 Penn Avenue South, Minneapolis, MN 55419.

Library of Congress Cataloging-in-Publication Data

Names: Koestler-Grack, Rachel A., 1973- author.
Title: Veterans Day / by Rachel Grack.
Description: Minneapolis, MN : Bellwether Media, Inc., [2018] | Series: Blastoff! Readers: Celebrating Holidays | Includes bibliographical references and index. | Audience: Grades K-3. | Audience: Ages 5-8.
Identifiers: LCCN 2016052739 (print) | LCCN 2016052970 (ebook) | ISBN 9781626176249 (hardcover : alk. paper) | ISBN 9781681033549 (ebook)
Subjects: LCSH: Veterans Day–Juvenile literature.
Classification: LCC D671 .K64 2018 (print) | LCC D671 (ebook) | DDC 394.264–dc23
LC record available at https://lccn.loc.gov/2016052739

Editor: Christina Leighton   Designer: Lois Stanfield

Printed in the United States of America, North Mankato, MN.

Table of Contents

Veterans Day Is Here!

Americans hang flags outside their houses. They think about the people who served the country.

They show **patriotism** at events.
It is **Veterans** Day!

What Is Veterans Day?

**Vietnam Veterans
Memorial**

This holiday honors the men
and women of the **military**.

People give respect to those who served in war and **peacetime**.

U.S. Armed Forces

United States Air Force

· · · · · · · · · · · · · · · ·

United States Army

· · · · · · · · · · · · · · · ·

United States Coast Guard

· · · · · · · · · · · · · · · ·

United States Marine Corps

· · · · · · · · · · · · · · · ·

United States Navy

Who Celebrates Veterans Day?

The United States celebrates Veterans Day.

Remembrance Day, Dartmouth, Canada

Other countries have a similar holiday. They call it Remembrance Day.

A peace agreement was signed on November 11, 1918. This ended the fighting in **World War I**.

The signing took place at 11:00 in the morning.

World War I cemetery in Flanders, Belgium

Americans wanted to remember this day of peace. They began celebrating **Armistice** Day.

U.S. soldiers on Armistice Day, 1918, France

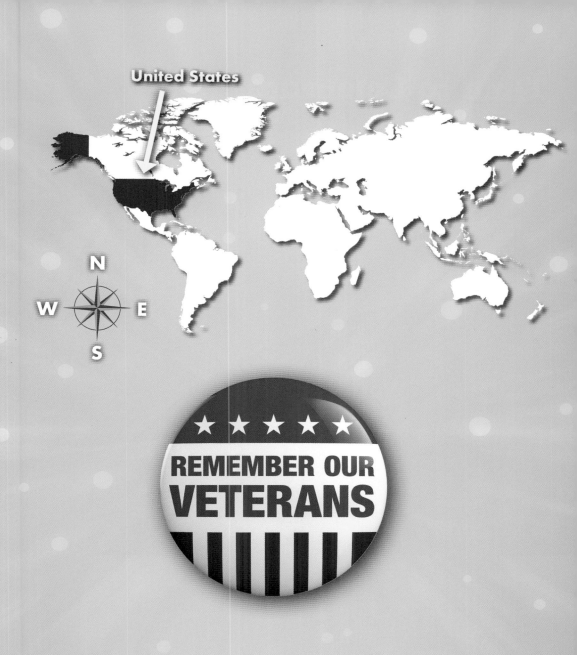

The United States changed the name to Veterans Day in 1954.

Veterans Day happens on November 11.

World War II memorial

Sometimes this day falls during the week. People often throw celebrations on the weekend.

Veterans Day Traditions!

Communities hold special parades. They invite veterans to march in their uniforms. Families wave flags and cheer.

Make an American Flag

Show patriotism with an American flag!

What You Need:
- red, white, and blue construction paper
- ruler
- pencil
- scissors
- glue
- small star stickers

What You Do:
1. Cut four 1-inch-wide strips lengthwise from the white construction paper.
2. Cut a 4-inch by 5-inch rectangle out of the blue construction paper.
3. Lay the red construction paper lengthwise.
4. Glue a white strip onto the red paper, 1 inch from the top.
5. Leave a 1-inch-wide red stripe. Then glue down the next white strip below it.
6. Repeat step 5 for the other two white strips.
7. Glue the blue rectangle in the upper left corner of the red-and-white striped paper.
8. Cover the blue rectangle with star stickers.

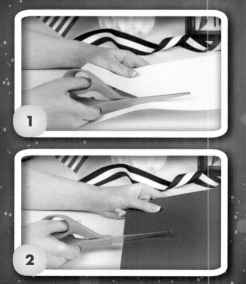

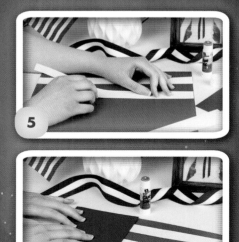

U.S. military and NATO forces in Afghanistan

Places across the world take two minutes of silence at 11:00 in the morning.

This quiet time shows respect for those who died in war.

veterans
in Canada

Some people go to the Veterans Day **National** Ceremony. The president lays a **wreath** on a special grave. A **bugler** plays **taps**.

President Obama, Veterans Day, 2013

bugler playing taps

Americans thank veterans
from the past and present!

Glossary

armistice—an agreement to stop fighting a war

bugler—someone who plays a bugle; a bugle is an instrument similar to a trumpet.

military—the armed forces

national—related to the entire country

patriotism—love, honor, and respect for one's country

peacetime—a time when a country is not at war

taps—the song played at military funerals and at night to signal bedtime

veterans—those who served in the armed forces

World War I—the war fought from 1914 to 1918 that involved many countries

wreath—leaves or flowers arranged in a circle as a sign of honor

To Learn More

AT THE LIBRARY
Dash, Meredith. *Veterans Day.* Minneapolis, Minn.: ABDO Kids, 2015.

Landau, Elaine. *What Is Veterans Day?* Berkeley Heights, N.J.: Enslow Publishers, 2012.

Pettiford, Rebecca. *Veterans Day.* Minneapolis, Minn.: Jump!, 2016.

ON THE WEB

Learning more about Veterans Day is as easy as 1, 2, 3.

1. Go to www.factsurfer.com.

2. Enter "Veterans Day" into the search box.

3. Click the "Surf" button and you will see a list of related web sites.

With factsurfer.com, finding more information is just a click away.

Index